W9-CGM-570

Defining
MOMENTS

Ellen
OCHOA

Reach for the Stars!

by Donna Latham

CONSULTANT
Michelle Nichols
Master Educator
Adler Planetarium & Astronomy Museum
Chicago, Illinois

BEARPORT
PUBLISHING COMPANY, INC.
New York, New York

Credits

Cover, NASA Johnson Space Center (NASA-JSC); Title page, NASA Johnson Space
Center (NASA-JSC); 4–5 (both), NASA Johnson Space Center (NASA-JSC);
6–7 (both), NASA Johnson Space Center (NASA-JSC); 8–9 (both) NASA Johnson
Space Center (NASA-JSC); 10–11 (both), NASA Johnson Space Center (NASA-
JSC); 12, Chuck Painter/Stanford News Service; 13, Linda A. Cicero/Stanford
News Service; 14–15 (both), NASA Johnson Space Center (NASA-JSC); 16, NASA
Johnson Space Center (NASA-JSC); 17, © 2005 SallyRideScience.com; 18–19
(both), NASA Johnson Space Center (NASA-JSC); 20–21 (both), NASA Johnson
Space Center (NASA-JSC); 22–23 (both), NASA Johnson Space Center (NASA-
JSC); 24, Courtesy of Worcester Polytechnic Institute; 25, NASA Johnson Space
Center (NASA-JSC); 26–27 (both), NASA Johnson Space Center (NASA-JSC).

Editorial development by Judy Nayer
Design by Fabia Wargin; Production by Luis Leon; Image Research by Jennifer Bright

Library of Congress Cataloging-in-Publication Data
Latham, Donna.
  Ellen Ochoa : reach for the stars! / by Donna Latham.
      p. cm. — (Defining moments)
  Includes bibliographical references and index.
  ISBN-13: 978-1-59716-076-6 (library binding)
  ISBN-10: 1-59716-076-8 (library binding)
  ISBN-13: 978-1-59716-113-8 (pbk.)
  ISBN-10: 1-59716-113-6 (pbk.)
  1. Ochoa, Ellen—Juvenile literature. 2. Women astronauts—United States—
Biography—Juvenile literature. 3. Astronauts—United States—Biography—
Juvenile literature. 4. Hispanic American women—Biography—Juvenile literature.
I. Title. II. Series: Defining moments (New York, N.Y.)

  TL789.85.O25L38 2006
  629.45'0092—dc22

                                    2005005332

For more information, write to Bearport Publishing Company, Inc.,
101 Fifth Avenue, Suite 6R, New York, New York 10003.
Printed in the United States of America.

10 9 8 7 6 5 4 3 2

Table of Contents

"Night into Day"

Excited friends and family waited at Kennedy Space Center. It was 1:30 a.m. on April 8, 1993. The space shuttle *Discovery* was ready to launch.

The final countdown began. "10, 9, 8, 7, 6, 5, 4, 3, 2, 1. Liftoff!" With an ear-splitting blast, *Discovery* roared into space.

Ellen Ochoa's first **mission** in space in 1993 was aboard *Discovery* shuttle flight STS-56.

Boosters help the space shuttle blast off. Ellen said the force and speed make you feel "like a gorilla is sitting on you."

Dr. Ellen Ochoa

Ellen Ochoa (oh-CHOH-ah) was strapped in on the flight deck. **Exhaust plumes** blazed across the **launch pad**. Ellen said it turned "night into day." In the dazzling light, Ellen became the world's first Hispanic woman in space.

Nine Days in Space

Ellen spent nine days on *Discovery*. She was excited to be part of such a talented crew. In space, Ellen could do research she "couldn't do anywhere else."

The crew of the STS-56 mission: (front row, from left) Commander Kenneth D. Cameron and Mission Specialist 1 C. Michael Foale; (back row, from left) Mission Specialist 3 Ellen Ochoa, Pilot Stephen S. Oswald, and Mission Specialist 2 Kenneth D. Cockrell.

A robotic arm can be moved joint by joint or with all the joints working together.

One of Ellen's jobs was controlling a **robotic arm**. First, Ellen used the 50-foot (15-m) arm to free the Spartan **satellite** from the shuttle. Spartan was being used to study the sun's outer **atmosphere**. Later, Ellen brought the satellite back to the shuttle.

Like a person's arm, the robotic arm has wrist, elbow, and shoulder joints. Hand controllers can be used to move it. "It's kind of like a video game," said Ellen.

"You Don't Need a Music Stand!"

A special job was planned for nearly every minute of *Discovery's* mission. Still, Ellen made time to play her flute.

Ellen had played since the age of ten. Playing in space, however, was a bit different.

Ellen plays her flute aboard Discovery.

Ellen never tires of looking out the window from space.

There is little **gravity** in space. As Ellen's body drifted, her sheet music floated before her. "You don't need a music stand!" Ellen joked. She gazed down at Earth as her music rang out.

"It was just very peaceful," Ellen later recalled. "It's a very fond memory."

While in space, Ellen also played on her flute "The Star-Spangled Banner" and, for Commander Ken Cameron, the "Marine Corps Hymn."

A Love of Learning

Ellen Ochoa was born on May 10, 1958, in Los Angeles, California. However, she calls La Mesa, California, her hometown.

Today, Ellen has a family of her own. She and her husband have two sons. The hardest part of her job is being away from her family.

Ellen's grandparents on her father's side **immigrated** to the United States from Mexico.

Ellen with her son (at right) and other crew members board a plane to the Johnson Space Center in Texas.

From a young age, Ellen was encouraged to do her best. One of five children, she was raised in a single-parent family. Her mother, Rosanne, had a deep love of learning. She passed it along to her children. Rosanne urged her children to try hard. Then, she told them, they could do anything.

It wasn't only Rosanne's words that **influenced** her children. Her actions were also important examples. While working to support the family, Rosanne went to college. In 22 years, she earned three degrees.

Top of Her Class

Ellen was an excellent student. Her favorite subjects were math and music. She completed high school at the top of her class. Then she moved on to college.

After college, Ellen attended Stanford University where she played flute in the school's orchestra.

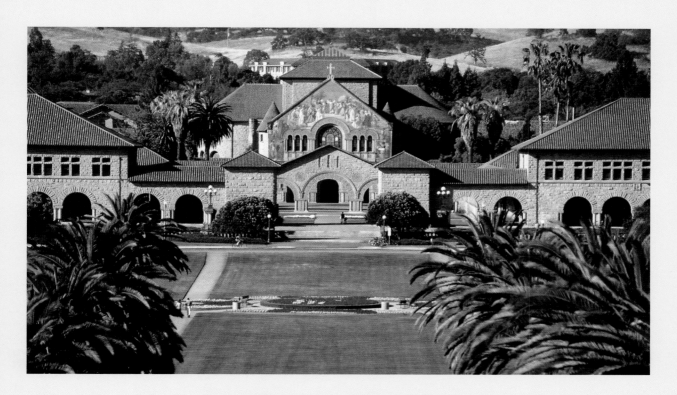

Stanford University in California

At first, Ellen didn't settle on a major, or main area of study. In fact, she changed her major five times. Ellen had many interests. She wanted to explore them all.

Then, a professor urged her to take a **physics** class. When she did, Ellen was hooked. With high honors, she graduated college with a physics degree in 1980.

By 1985, Ellen had earned a master's degree and a **doctorate** in electrical engineering from Stanford University.

13

"It Never Occurred to Me..."

On July 20, 1969, 500 million people around the world were glued to their televisions. They watched in amazement as astronaut Neil Armstrong made the first historic step onto the moon. Ellen was 11 years old.

"That's one small step for man, one giant leap for mankind."

—*Neil Armstrong, July 20, 1969*

People around the world were riveted by Neil Armstrong's walk on the moon.

Many astronauts had dreamed of going into space when they were children. For Ellen it was different.

"It never occurred to me that I could grow up and be an astronaut," Ellen explained. For many boys, an astronaut was a **career** choice. It wasn't the same for girls. In 1969, there were few women scientists. There were no women astronauts. Girls lacked the **role models** they have today.

Even when Ellen set off for college in the 1970s, there were still few jobs for women in math and science. Many people believed women weren't suited for those jobs.

Applying to NASA

By 1983, times were finally changing! That year, Sally Ride became the first American woman in space.

In 1985, Ellen worked as an **engineer** and inventor. At that time, some friends applied for astronaut jobs. They pointed out that Ellen's skills were the right stuff for NASA.

NASA stands for *National Aeronautics and Space Administration.* NASA is always accepting astronaut applications.

On June 18, 1983, Sally Ride became the first American woman in space.

Today, the Sally Ride Science Club holds festivals for middle-school girls. Sally encourages girls to consider science careers.

Suddenly, Ellen realized she could be an astronaut. She applied to NASA's astronaut program, too. Would she be chosen?

It wasn't like Ellen to just sit and wait. In the meantime, she landed a new job at NASA's Ames Research Center. She even learned to fly a plane for fun. Soon she earned a private pilot's license.

Training for Space

In January 1990, Ellen received exciting news. NASA had chosen her! She kicked off the new year by moving to Houston, Texas. There she joined others to train at the Johnson Space Center.

Ellen learned water survival skills.

After her training, Ellen officially became an astronaut in 1991.

Ellen also went through wilderness survival training.

Training was tough on the mind and the body. Ellen took classes in geology, medicine, and physics. She learned flight and survival skills.

Shuttle landings are supposed to take place on land. Unfortunately, that's not where they always happen. So astronauts train to be ready for anything that might go wrong.

Ellen prepared for emergency landings. She learned to parachute. During water survival training, she floated in full gear.

Zero-G and the Vomit Comet

In space, Ellen lives and works where there is little gravity. There is so little that astronauts call it zero gravity, or zero-G.

In zero-G, people become **weightless**. Their bodies float in any direction. "This," said Ellen, "is the fun part of a mission."

Astronauts in training discover what it's like to be weightless in the Vomit Comet.

The KC-135

To train for working in zero-G, Ellen rode the KC-135. The powerful jet soared high in a curve. Then it suddenly dropped down—nearly two miles (3 km). For 25 seconds, Ellen became weightless. The up-and-down pattern was repeated 40 times in three hours.

Astronauts compare the stomach-sloshing ride to a roller coaster. They jokingly call the KC-135 "the Vomit Comet."

When film director Ron Howard made the movie *Apollo 13*, he borrowed the KC-135. His actors shot their weightless scenes in the Vomit Comet.

Spending Time in Space

Today, Ellen has logged nearly 1,000 hours in space. Her second mission was STS-66 on the space shuttle *Atlantis* in 1994. The crew continued their earlier studies of the atmosphere.

On the space shuttle, Ellen uses a camera to record an ocean scene.

Ellen aboard Discovery *in 1999*

In 1999, Ellen blasted off on *Discovery* for mission STS-96. For five days, the shuttle was docked to the International Space Station (ISS). Ellen was in charge of moving supplies aboard.

Ellen returned to the ISS on *Atlantis* in 2002 for mission STS-110. Again she worked with a robotic arm. This time, she used the station's robotic arm to move fellow astronauts around as they did jobs in space.

The first crew moved into the ISS in 2000. They used the supplies Ellen had left for them.

A Chance to Give Back

Ellen feels that being Hispanic has given her a chance to give back to the community. She often speaks to Hispanic groups and to schools.

In 2003, Ellen spoke to students graduating from college. She told them the best part of her job is working closely with talented people.

Launch and landing are the riskiest times on space flights. Training, Ellen says, helps her feel prepared to deal with the risks.

Ellen speaks to a graduating class.

24

Ellen shared a tragic part of her work, too. It was the death of her friend, Rick Husband. That year, he died on the space shuttle *Columbia*.

Ellen swore there was no other place the doomed crew wanted to be. She believes that there's nothing else astronauts would rather be dedicating their lives to.

Tragically, the Columbia crew never returned home. The shuttle broke up over north-central Texas during its reentry.

A Role Model

As a girl, Ellen couldn't look to American women astronauts as role models. There weren't any. Today, Ellen realizes she has become a role model herself. She has found a place in history.

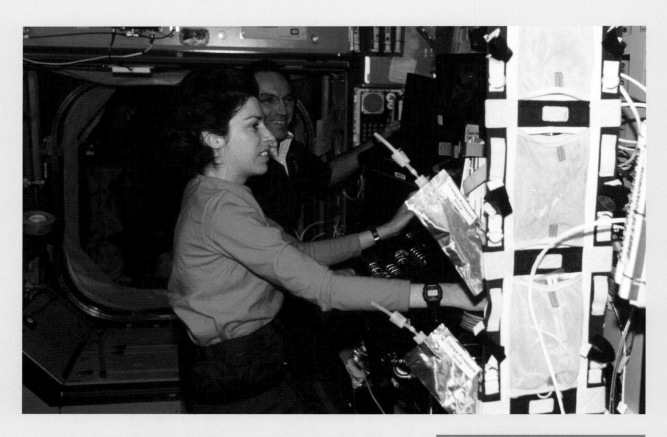

Two missions took Ellen to the ISS. Here Ellen operates the controls of the robotic arm.

Ellen Ochoa Middle School opened in 2002. It is located in Pasco, Washington.

Ellen's education was her launch pad. It blasted her into space. When she visits schools, Ellen tells students about her lifelong love of learning. She urges them to get good educations.

"Don't be afraid to reach for the stars," Ellen says. "I believe a good education can take you anywhere on Earth and beyond."

Ellen Ochoa has done much more than reach for the stars. She has soared among them.

Just the Facts

■ Ellen calls her mother, Rosanne, her greatest role model. They were college students at the same time. Rosanne graduated from San Diego State University in 1982—two years after Ellen completed her degree.

■ Ellen has earned many awards. Among them are NASA's Outstanding Leadership Medal (1995) and Exceptional Service Medal (1997). She has also won the Hispanic Heritage Leadership Award.

Timeline

Here are some important events in the life of Ellen Ochoa.

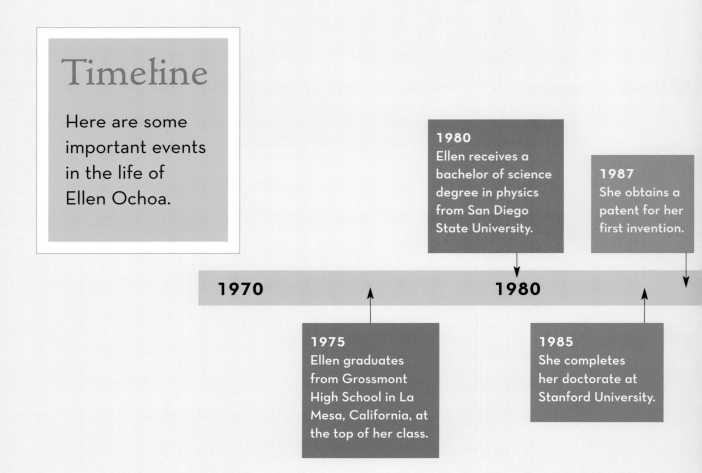

1980
Ellen receives a bachelor of science degree in physics from San Diego State University.

1987
She obtains a patent for her first invention.

1970

1980

1975
Ellen graduates from Grossmont High School in La Mesa, California, at the top of her class.

1985
She completes her doctorate at Stanford University.

■ Among many interests, Ellen enjoys hiking, bicycling, volleyball, and playing her flute. "If you are motivated to excel in one area," she says, "you are usually motivated to excel in others. NASA looks for that."

■ It's hard for Ellen to be away from her family when she's on a mission. To stay in touch, she e-mails her husband from space each day. Sometimes she holds video conferences to connect with her family on Earth.

■ Ellen is now the deputy director of flight crew operations at the Johnson Space Center.

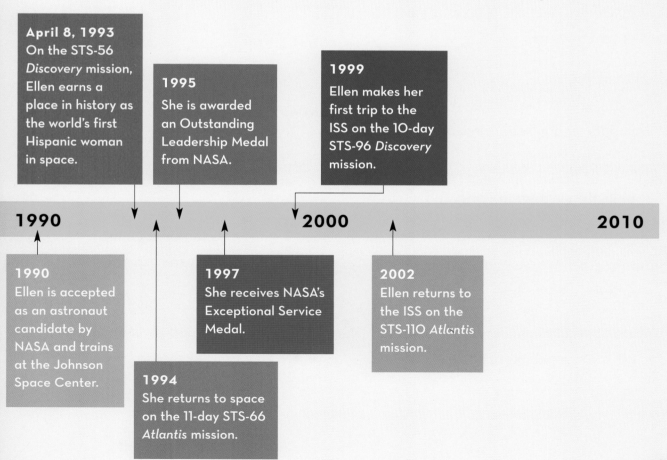

April 8, 1993
On the STS-56 *Discovery* mission, Ellen earns a place in history as the world's first Hispanic woman in space.

1995
She is awarded an Outstanding Leadership Medal from NASA.

1999
Ellen makes her first trip to the ISS on the 10-day STS-96 *Discovery* mission.

1990

2000

2010

1990
Ellen is accepted as an astronaut candidate by NASA and trains at the Johnson Space Center.

1997
She receives NASA's Exceptional Service Medal.

2002
Ellen returns to the ISS on the STS-110 *Atlantis* mission.

1994
She returns to space on the 11-day STS-66 *Atlantis* mission.

Glossary

atmosphere (AT-muhss-fihr) the mixture of gases surrounding Earth

career (kuh-RIHR) a job or profession engaged in over a long period of time

doctorate (DOK-tur-ut) the highest university degree, also called a Ph.D.

engineer (en-juh-NIHR) someone who is trained in the use or design of machines, engines, bridges, roads, or other structures

exhaust plumes (eg-ZAWST PLOOMZ) rising smoke that results when fumes, vapors, and gases are released at liftoff

gravity (GRAV-uh-tee) the force that pulls things toward Earth and keeps them from drifting into space

immigrated (IM-uh-grate-ud) came to a new country to live

influenced (IN-floo-uhnssd) had an effect on a person or thing

launch pad (LAWNCH PAD) the platform from which a spacecraft is sent into space

mission (MISH-uhn) a certain job to be performed

physics (FIZ-iks) the science that deals with matter and energy, including the study of light, heat, sound, motion, electricity, and force

robotic arm (roh-BOT-ik ARM) mechanical arm

role models (ROHL MOD-uhlz) people who are held up as examples or inspirations

satellite (SAT-uh-*lite*) a spacecraft that is sent into orbit in space in order to send information back to Earth

weightless (WATE-liss) having very little or no weight, especially because of little gravity

Bibliography

Cooper, Henry S. F. *Before Liftoff: The Making of a Space Shuttle Crew.* Baltimore, MD: The Johns Hopkins University Press (1987).

Posada-Swafford, Angela. "A Place in the Stars." *Latina* 16, no. 6 (2003).

Reichhardt, Tony. *Space Shuttle: The First Twenty Years—Astronauts' Experiences in Their Own Words.* New York: DK Publishing (2002).

Woodmansee, Laura S. *Women Astronauts.* Burlington, Ontario, Canada: Apogee Books (2002).

Read More

Iverson, Teresa. *Ellen Ochoa (Hispanic-American Biographies).* Chicago, IL: Raintree (2005).

Paige, Joy. *Ellen Ochoa: The First Hispanic Woman in Space.* New York: Rosen Publishing Group (2004).

Romero, Maritza. *Ellen Ochoa: The First Hispanic Woman Astronaut.* New York: PowerKids Press (1997).

St. John, Jetty. *Hispanic Scientists: Ellen Ochoa, Carlos A. Ramírez, Eloy Rodriguez, Lydia Villa-Komaroff, Maria Elena Zavala.* Mankato, MN: Capstone (1996).

Learn More Online

Visit these Web sites to learn more about Ellen Ochoa and astronauts:

astronauts.nasa.gov/
teacher.scholastic.com/activities/hispanic/ochoatscript.htm
www.nasa.gov/home/hqnews/2003/jun/HQ_03207_Ochoa_1st.html
www1.edspace.nasa.gov/text/astroschool/survival/

Index

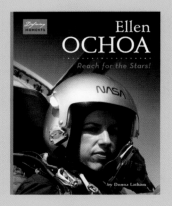

About the Author

A former school librarian, **DONNA LATHAM** is a writer in the Chicago, Illinois, area. One of her favorite childhood memories is of watching the *Apollo 11* moon landing on TV.

DATE DUE			

B
OCH

Latham, Donna.

**Ellen Ochoa : reach
for the stars!**

**FRANKLIN ELEMENTARY SCHOOL
MEDIA CENTER**